My Rare Animal 123

Marcus Davies

Text by Brian Moses

WWF

About the illustrator
London born Marcus Davies grew up in Jersey, Channel Islands. He studied fashion and textiles at Saint Martin's School of Art, London, graduating with a final collection inspired by a scholarship trip to Brazil. He now works as a freelance designer in his trained fields. *My Rare Animal 123* is one of two WWF UK books illustrated by Marcus using a paper collage technique.

To Mum, Dad, Adam and Michael
for their constant support

Acknowledgement
Paper for original artwork was Keay Kolour antique finish, supplied by Arjo Wiggins Fine Papers, Paperpoint, 130 Long Acre, Covent Garden, London.

First published in 1992 by
WWF UK (World Wide Fund For Nature)
Panda House
Weyside Park
Godalming
Surrey GU7 1XR

ISBN 0 947613 51 X

Printed in the UK

1

Huge herds of **AMERICAN BISON** once roamed the plains of North America. Now they live in national parks where they are protected.

2

KIWIS are found in the forests of North Island, New Zealand. They are shy creatures and cannot fly. Their keen sense of smell helps them to sniff out food.

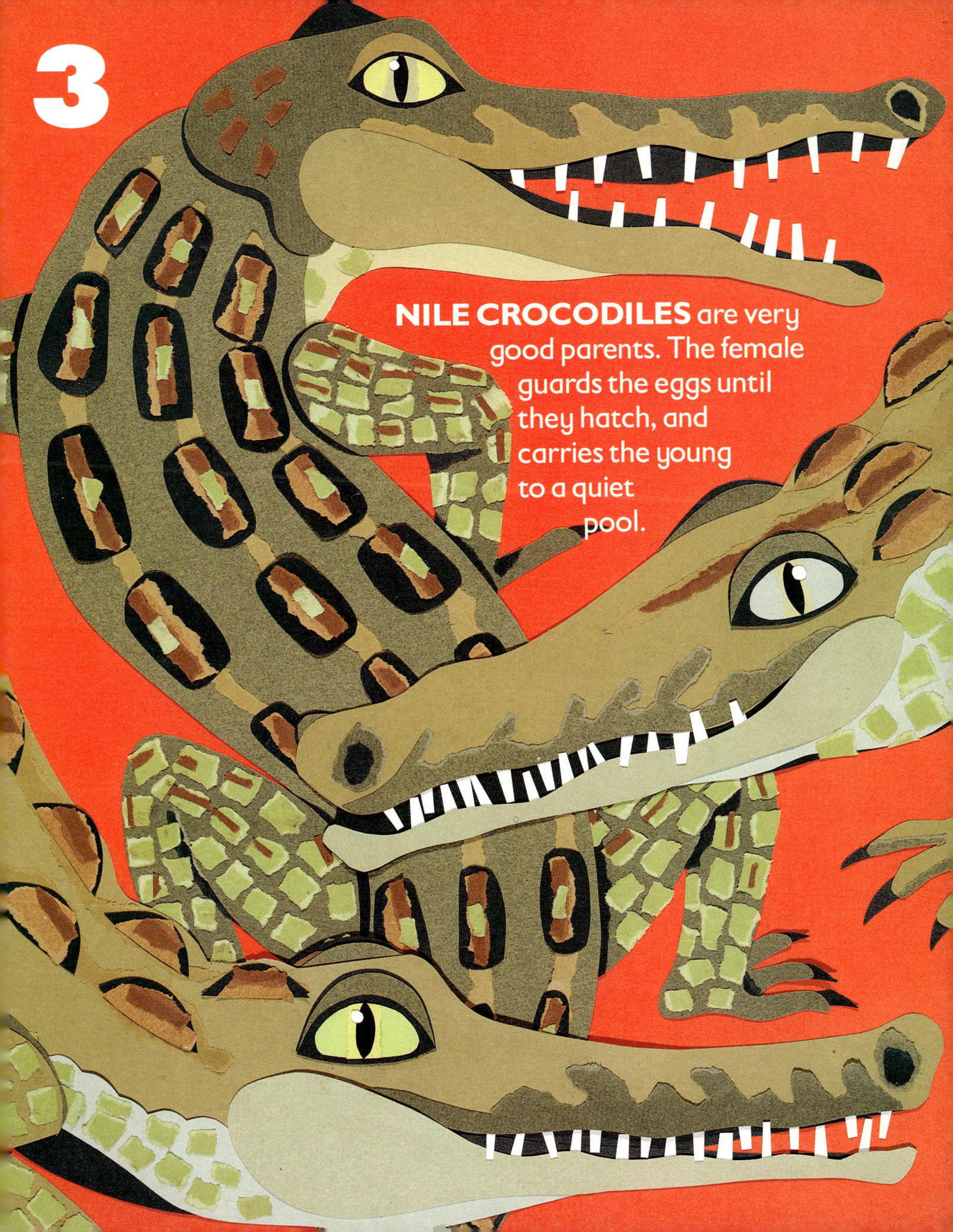

3

NILE CROCODILES are very good parents. The female guards the eggs until they hatch, and carries the young to a quiet pool.

4

POLAR BEARS live in Arctic regions of ice and snow. They feed mainly on seals and wait to catch them at holes in the ice where seals surface to breathe.

SNOW LEOPARDS are shy animals. The colour of their coat helps them to hide among the rocks and snow of their mountain home in Central Asia.

6

GORILLAS live in the rainforests of Central Africa. Young gorillas like to play like humans do. They climb trees, swing on branches and chase each other.

7

MANATEES are gentle, slow-moving plant-eaters. They live in warm shallow seas and rivers along the American coast and are often called sea-cows.

8 **TOUCANS** have brightly-coloured beaks which can often be longer than their body.

They use their beaks
to reach fruit hanging at
the end of a branch.

FRUIT BATS are known as 'flying foxes'.

In the day they hang upside down in trees, but at dusk they fly off to look for fruit.

10 Herds of **WILD HORSES** once roamed the plains of Mongolia. Each herd was made up of a stallion and 5 or 6 mares.

11

GIANT OTTERS have large flat feet. This makes walking difficult and they spend less time on land than most other otters! They like to eat small catfish and piranhas.

GOLDEN LION TAMARINS may look like small lions, but they are really monkeys. They leap from branch to branch, holding on with their long fingers.

13

SNOWY OWLS live in cold northern lands. Their soft, loose feathers allow the owls to fly silently and take lemmings and hares by surprise.

At nesting time **GREEN TURTLES** from Brazil travel over 2,000 kilometres to Ascension Island to lay their eggs. Each female lays about 100 eggs, but only a few survive.

There are about 300 different kinds of **PARROTS** in the world. Most are brightly coloured, and their powerful bills can crush the hardest nuts and seeds.

ANACONDAS are completely deaf. They rely on sight and smell to catch their prey.

WHOOPING CRANES make a loud noise that can be heard up to 4 kilometres away. They prefer to eat shellfish which they catch with one sharp jab of their beak.

TREE FROGS have suckers on their toes which allow them to spend much of their time in the treetops. Their bright colours warn other creatures that they are not good to eat.

PENGUINS have a thick layer of fat and tightly packed feathers to help keep them warm. They are clumsy on land, but fast and skilful in water.

The **QUEEN ALEXANDRA'S BIRDWING BUTTERFLY** is one of the largest and heaviest butterflies in the world. Can you also see the beautiful **BLUE MORPHO?**